Be My Guest

a handbook to dining etiquette

written and illustrated by Elise Oppenheim

recipes contributed by Kristine McWherter Cornelius

© Copyright Elise Oppenheim
All rights reserved

Table of Contents

Introduction	1
The Table Setting	2
Placement	3
Salt and Pepper	5
Wine	6
Let's Be Seated	7
The Soup Course	11
Bread	17
The Fish Course	20
Sorbet	27
The Meat Course	28
The Salad Course	34
The Dessert Course	39
End of the Meal	44
Challenging Foods	48
Pasta	51
Artichoke	52
French Fries	57
Peas	59
Corn on the Cob	61
Asparagus	62

Recipes

Mushroom Bisque 14

French Onion Soup 15

Herb Butter 19

Poached Salmon 23

Breaded Halibut with Aioli 24

Filet Mignon 31

Stuffed Cornish Hens 32

Caesar Salad 36

Citrus Salad with Basil Dressing 37

Watermelon Feta Salad 38

Tiramisu 41

Chocolate Mousse 43

Marinara Sauce for Pasta 51

Steamed Artichokes 53

Roasted Artichokes 54

Sweet Potato Fries 58

Roasted Asparagus 63

Squash Souffle 64

Green Beans Almondine 65

Brussels Sprouts 66

Introduction

Proper etiquette separates the sophisticated from the rogue. Well-mannered ladies and gentleman are more respected and are apt to go farther professionally. A well-set table is an art but can seem very intimidating. It is actually very simple once you learn the basics. There are numerous designs in table setting. However, we will focus on one design commonly used in formal dining. One rule of thumb – work from the outside in.

This handbook features suggested recipes for each course so you can host your own dinner party to practice proper table manners at home. Turn off your cell phones (an absolute dining *faux pas*) and join me in an adventure in dining. You are invited to *be my guest*.

The Table Setting

All silverware should align the bottom of the service plate, also referred to as the charger plate. This plate is removed before the first course and replaced with a dinner plate. The bread plate is placed directly above the dinner fork with the butter knife placed across and facing left.

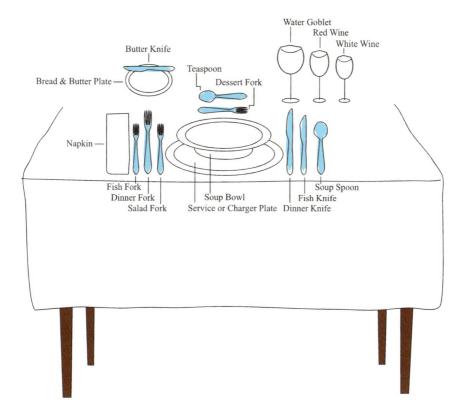

The teaspoon and dessert fork in this design go directly above the service plate. All glasses are placed on the right side with the water glass being first, followed by the glass for red wine and then white. The water glass is directly above the dinner knife. Any food dish to the left is yours and any glass to the right is yours.

Placement

Fork on top of knife in a criss cross position, prongs facing down, signifies you are not finished with your meal. This is known as the "rest" position.

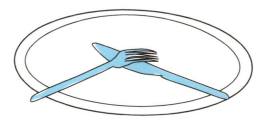

Fork resting to left of knife with prongs facing down, signifies you are finished with your meal. Blade of knife faces inward, and both utensils are at 4:20 on plate.

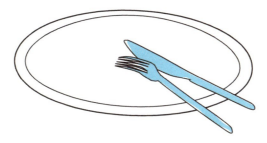

If you are using only the fork, then you would place it prongs side up when finished.

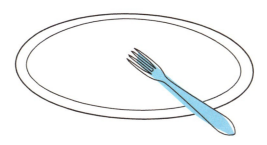

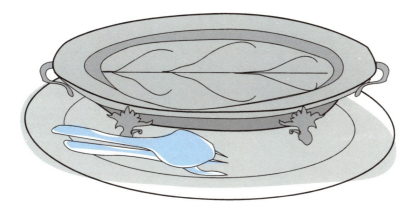

When finished serving, place spoon on fork with prongs facing down on side of platter.

Salt and Pepper

Salt and pepper shakers are *always* passed together as a pair.

Wine

Wine glasses are always held by the stem. Touching the bowl of the glass can alter the temperature of the wine. The server ALWAYS pours. Ladies never pour their own wine. The gentleman can pour for the lady if the server is not around. If you are not drinking, just place your hand over the top of the glass.

Let's Be Seated

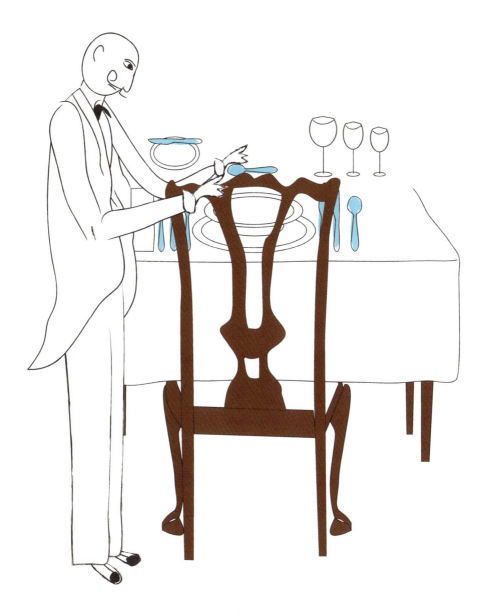

Gentlemen pull out the chair to seat the lady unless she is seated first by the host. Immediately unfold napkin and place in your lap. Do not shake it out and never wear your napkin like a bib. Engage in conversation and do not look around the room at others or find distractions. If the lady needs to excuse herself from the table, the gentleman always stands up.

If you are at a dinner party, the gentleman will assist the lady on his right to be seated. Remember, wait until the host or hostess begins eating before you start.

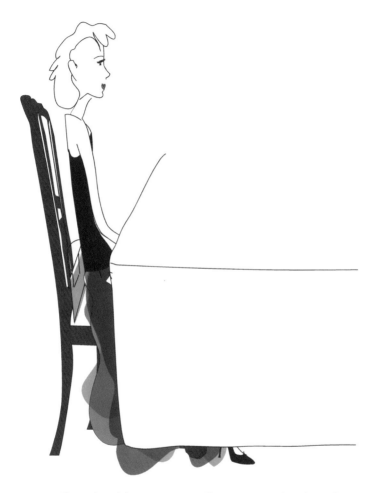

Ladies should carry a small purse or clutch. A large, bulky bag is too cumbersome. It is not proper to place your personal items on the table. If there is not an extra chair for your handbag, put it behind you on your chair or underneath the napkin on your lap. Do not put it on the floor.

It is impolite to rest your elbows on the table. You can rest your wrists and forearms on the edge of the table or simply keep them in your lap. Fidgeting with your hair is a no-no.

The Soup Course

Soup is the first course. Use the spoon on your outer right.

Soup can be tricky, and it can certainly make an impression. If you dip a piece of bread in your soup, put your spoon down on the under plate and use your soup hand. If crackers are brought to the table that are larger than bite size, do not crumble them in the soup. Use your hands to eat them.

Always glide the spoon in the bowl away from you.

Do not blow on your soup, slurp or put the entire spoon in your mouth. Delicately sip your soup with the edge of the spoon facing you.

When you are finished with your soup lay the spoon across the upper righthand corner of your plate, bowl side up.

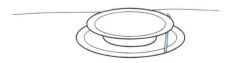

Mushroom Bisque

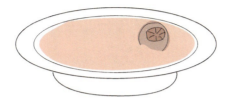

Ingredients

1/4 cup butter
1 lb mushrooms, sliced
3 shallots, minced
1/4 cup flour
1/2 tsp salt
1 cup chicken broth
3 cups half-and-half cream
1 tbsp lemon juice
salt and pepper to taste
fresh parsley

Melt butter in saucepan. Cook mushrooms and shallots until tender, about 10 minutes. Add flour and salt. Gradually stir in broth and half-and-half. Continue stirring and cook about 5 minutes. Add lemon juice and season to taste. Garnish with parsley. (Serves 4)

French Onion Soup

Ingredients

4 large onions, thinly sliced
4 tbsp butter
40 oz beef broth
1/2 cup dry sherry (optional)
2 tsp Worcestershire sauce
dash of pepper
6 slices French bread toasted
6 slices or 12 oz grated Swiss cheese

Cook onions in butter until translucent. Add broth, sherry, Worcestershire sauce and pepper. Bring to a boil. Divide into 6 ovenproof bowls or crocks. Place a slice of French bread into each and top with cheese. Put under the broiler and heat until cheese bubbles. (Serves 6)

Always wipe the corner of your mouth with your napkin before taking a drink of water.

Bread

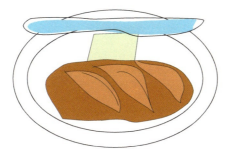

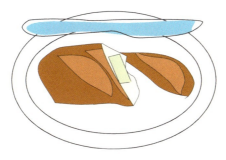

Bread and butter are placed on the table. Tear off a piece of bread and eat in small bites. The bread and butter plate and knife will remain on the table after soup bowls are removed.

At a dinner party, you pass to the left, and the table is cleared from the right. It is not polite to reach over the table.

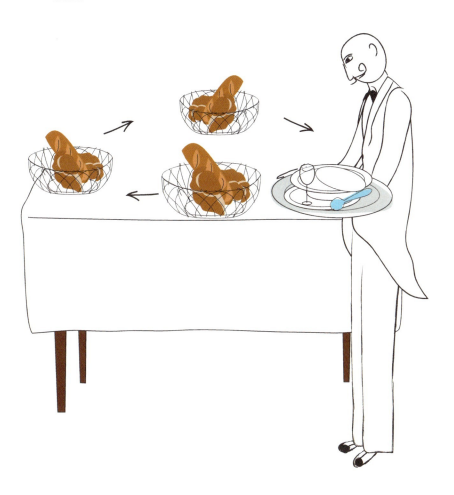

Herb Butter

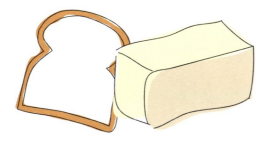

Ingredients

2 sticks butter, softened
Herbs, chopped:
1 bay leaf
3 tbsp garlic chives
3 tbsp parsley
1 sage leaf
1 tbsp oregano
1 tbsp basil
1 tbsp thyme

Mix herbs with softened butter. Make sure all of the herbs are incorporated well. Put mixture in plastic wrap and roll into a log, twisting the ends. Then wrap in foil and twist again. Put into the freezer until hardened. Then slice pieces when needed.

The Fish Course

Fish is the second course. Use the fork on the outer left and the knife on the outer right.

Pick up the serving fork with your right hand, the serving spoon with your left. Keep your arms parallel and sit up straight. Place the serving pieces on the right side of the serving dish, fork on bottom and spoon on top of fork. Bowl of the spoon faces down.

Fish bones are removed with your fingers from your mouth.

The fish knife is not held the same way as the dinner knife. This is because you are not actually cutting the fish. You are merely breaking it apart. Hold the knife between your thumb and your index and middle fingers.

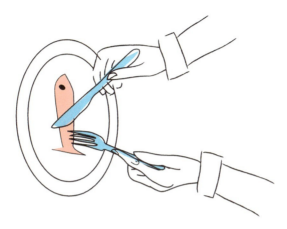

Hold the fork in your left hand, prongs down. Continue to hold the knife in your right hand. If it is not necessary to use the fish knife, the fork is held in the *right* hand, prongs facing up or down. Leave knife on the table.

Poached Salmon

Ingredients

1/2 lb salmon per person
1 cup white wine
3 cups chicken broth
1 lemon, sliced
1 bunch scallions, chopped
1 cup heavy cream or yogurt
1 cup frozen peas
2 tbsp tomato paste

In a deep saute pan make poaching liquid with white wine, chicken broth, juice from 1/2 lemon, and chopped scallions. When liquid is gently boiling add fillets. Cover and cook until the pink becomes lighter, about 3 or 4 minutes. Remove fish when done and place in the oven to keep warm.

Reduce the liquid to half by boiling. Add cream, tomato paste and peas. Cook down to sauce-like consistency. Place salmon fillets on a platter, and pour sauce over them. Garnish with lemon slices.

Breaded Halibut with Aioli

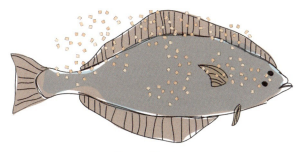

Ingredients

2 lbs fresh halibut fillets
1/2 cup Panko bread crumbs
1/2 cup flour
olive oil
1/2 cup parsley, chopped
1 tsp cayenne pepper or red pepper flakes
1 egg
salt and black pepper
Aioli:
1/2 cup Greek yogurt
1 tbsp mayonnaise
1 or 2 garlic cloves, crushed
1 lemon
1 tbsp fresh dill, chopped

Combine Panko, hot pepper flakes, some lemon zest, parsley, salt and black pepper in a bowl. Set aside.

Crack the egg and beat it lightly. Dip halibut in the egg, then sprinkle and pat with flour. Next, dredge the halibut with the Panko mixture.

Lightly coat skillet with olive oil and put on medium heat. When the pan is fairly hot, cook the fish, skin side up, until the pan side turns white. Flip the fish and cook until the meat is white all the way through.

Mix the ingredients for the aioli, using juice from half a lemon, and whisk. Pour in a serving bowl with a spoon. Any leftover lemon and parlsey can be used as a garnish for your fish.

Don't gesticulate with your untensils or speak with your mouth full of food.

Don't lick your fingers or eating utensils.

Sorbet

A scoop of sorbet (pronounced sor-bet or sor-bay) is sometimes served in between courses to clean the palate.

The Meat Course

Meat is the third course. Use the dinner fork, outer left, and the dinner knife.

Take small bites and chew with your mouth closed. Never hold your utensils up while talking. Taste your food first before adding salt and pepper. It is extremely rude to season before tasting. Gristle is removed with your fingers from your mouth.

The meat knife is held with the forefinger pointing down on the handle. Cut one bite at a time.

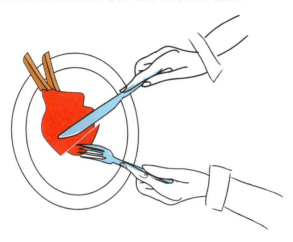

Hold the fork in your left hand, prongs down, with the forefinger pointing down on the handle. Continue to hold the knife in your right hand.

Filet Mignon

Ingredients

2 tenderloin filets 4 to 6 oz (1 to 1/2 inches thick)
extra virgin olive oil
salt and pepper to taste
herb butter (page 19)

Bring filets to room temperature. Preheat oven to 400 degrees. Rub filets with olive oil and season with a little salt and pepper. Heat an oven-safe skillet on medium to high. When the pan is hot, sear the filets for 2 or 3 minutes on each side, turning only once. Then place pan with filets in oven for 6 to 10 minutes, or until the desired doneness is achieved. Transfer them to a plate, and top with a pat of herb butter.

Rare - 120 degrees
Medium Rare - 125 degrees
Medium - 130 degrees

Stuffed Cornish Hens

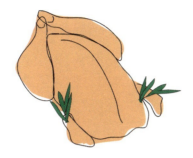

Ingredients

2 cornish hens
1/3 cup uncooked long grain rice
3/4 cup chicken broth
1/2 cup mushrooms, chopped
2 tbsp slivered almonds
2 tbsp onion, finely chopped
3 tbsp butter, divided
2 tbsp lemon juice
1/2 tsp salt, divided
1/8 tsp black pepper

In a saucepan, cook and stir rice, onion and almonds in 2 tbsp. butter over medium heat. Cook until rice is slightly browned (about 5 minutes). Stir in chicken broth, lemon juice and 1/4 tsp. salt. Bring to a boil. Reduce heat. Cover and simmer for 15 minutes or until rice is tender. Stir in mushrooms.

Sprinkle the outside and inner cavity of hens with pepper and remaining salt. Stuff hens with rice mixture and place on oven rack in a shallow roasting pan coated with non-stick cooking spray. Melt the remaining butter and brush over hens. Cover and bake at 400 degrees for 25-35 minutes or until juices run clear. Your meat thermometer should read 180 degrees for the hens and 165 degrees for the stuffing. Serve on a platter garnished with sprigs of a fresh herb.

The Salad Course

The salad is the fourth course. Use the remaining fork, which is broader than the other ones.

The salad fork is shaped a little differently from the other forks. This makes it easier for cutting. When you are finished with your salad, the bread & butter plates, along with the wine glasses, will be taken away to make room for dessert.

Caesar Salad

Ingredients

Romaine lettuce

croutons

Parmesan cheese

Dressing:

1/2 cup olive oil

1-2 garlic cloves, crushed

1 egg

1/2 can anchovies or anchovy paste

1 tsp lemon juice

1 tsp Worcestershire sauce

1 tbsp red wine vinegar

Wash lettuce thoroughly and dry. Cut off bottom ends of leaves and break into bite size pieces. Whisk dressing ingredients in a bowl. Add lettuce and toss gently. Top with Parmesan and croutons.

Citrus Salad with Basil Dressing

Ingredients

1 grapefruit, peeled and cut into slices
2 oranges, peeled and cut into slices
1/2 red onion, peeled and thinly sliced
1/3 cup pitted black olives, chopped or sliced
Dressing:
1 bunch fresh basil leaves, thinly sliced (1 cup)
2 tbsp chopped chives
3 tbsp balsamic vinegar
3 tbsp extra virgin olive oil

Place fruit slices on a serving platter. Sprinkle onion slices on top. Then sprinkle olives. Process dressing ingredients in a blender and drizzle over salad. Serve.

Watermelon Feta Salad

Ingredients

4 oz feta cheese, cut into bite sizes

2 lbs watermelon, scooped into balls

8 oz grape tomatoes, cut in halves

3 tbsp extra virgin olive oil

1/2 tsp fresh mint, finely chopped

2 tsp white balsamic vinegar

1/2 tsp kosher salt

3 cups arugula greens

1 cup red onion, sliced

Whisk olive oil, vinegar and salt to blend. Set aside. Place arugula, mint, onions and tomatoes in a salad bowl. Add vinegar mixture. Toss to coat. Add feta cheese and melon (Serves 6)

The Dessert Course

Dessert is the fifth course. Use the dessert spoon above your plate if eating fruit or ice cream. Use the fork above your plate if eating cake.

Small dessert plates will be brought to the table along with coffee or tea cups. The water glass is the only stemware that remains on the table.

Dessert wines are sometimes served, such as port or brandy.

Tiramisu

Ingredients

3 large eggs, whites and yolks separated

1/2 cup sugar

8 oz mascarpone cheese

20 lady fingers

1 cup espresso or strong coffee

2 tbsp brandy or cognac

1/8 cup cocoa

Combine 3 egg yolks, 1 tbsp espresso or coffee, sugar and cognac or brandy into a large mixing bowl. Beat 2 or 3 minutes. Add mascarpone cheese and beat 3 to 5 minutes until you have a smooth consistency. In a separate bowl combine 3 egg whites and a pinch of sugar. Beat until mixture forms stiff peaks. Gently fold into the mascarpone mixture.

Pour rest of espresso or coffee into a flat dish and dip one side of each lady finger and layer on bottom of a flat dish. Spread 1/3 of mascarpone mixture and sprinkle

with cocoa. Continue layering lady fingers, mascarpone mixture and cocoa until you end with the top layer being mixture and cocoa. Refrigerate 1 hour before serving.

Chocolate Mousse

Ingredients

2 oz unsweetened chocolate, melted

2 cups whipping cream

1/2 cup powdered sugar

1/8 tsp salt

1 tsp vanilla or almond extract

Whip cream, sugar and salt together until stiff. Add chocolate and flavored extract, mixing well. Chill in refrigerator or freezer. Serve in champagne glasses or on top of fruit or cake. You can also top with whipped cream and garnish with mint leaves.

End of the Meal

When the meal has been completed, place your napkin to the left of your plate. Never put it in your chair. Do not fold it or crumple it up. Silverware that was used is placed at 4:20 on plate. Unused utensils remain in their proper position.

If your server brings you a dipping bowl after the meal, delicately dip you fingers in the water and dry your hands with your napkin. Don't wash your hands in the bowl as you would under a faucet.

If you must use a toothpick, excuse yourself from the table.

Never tell everyone where you are going. Just say "Excuse me. I will be back shortly." This also applies to women and makeup.

Never push your plate away from you and never leave your chair sticking out.

Challenging Foods

There are some foods that can be quite intimidating. Once you become familiar with art of eating them, you will find they are "a piece of cake."

Pasta

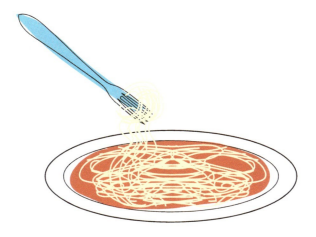

Pick up several strands of pasta with your fork and twirl it around your fork. Don't cut it into little pieces and don't overload your fork.

Never, ever slurp.

Marinara Sauce for Pasta

Ingredients

4 garlic cloves, minced
1/4 cup shallots, minced
1/4 cup extra virgin olive oil
5 lbs very ripe tomatoes (15-20)
  seeded and chopped or canned
  stewed tomatoes (40-oz)
1 bunch fresh basil, chopped
salt and pepper to taste

Saute garlic and shallots in 2 tbsp olive oil. Combine tomatoes, basil, salt and pepper. Add remaining olive oil and bring to a boil, stirring often. Reduce heat to a simmer and cook in a covered pan for 1-3 hours. Serve with your favorite *al dente* pasta and top with fresh grated Parmesan cheese.

Artichoke

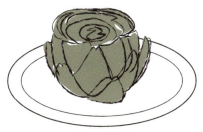

Tear off a leaf, starting from the outside, and dip the broad part that has the meat of the leaf into the sauce. It could be a salad dressing or even drawn butter.

Hold with your fingers and pull off the meaty end with your teeth. Discard the rest of the leaf into bowl. That part is not eaten.

When you get to the exremely thin leaves, pull them off as a bunch and scrape out the silky choke with your spoon. Then proceed to cut the heart with your knife and fork.

Steamed Artichokes

Ingredients

2 whole artichokes
1 quart chicken broth
1/4 cup white wine
4 garlic cloves
2 lemons, cut in halves
4 sprigs parsley
2 bay leaves
2 tbsp olive oil
salt and pepper to taste

Combine parsley, garlic, bay leaves, lemons, olive oil, and broth in a large pot and bring to a simmer. Season liquid with salt and pepper. Wash artichokes under cold water. Cut off stems at base and pull off lower leaves. Cut off top inch of artichoke. Trim thorny tips of petals with kitchen shears. Put artichokes in the pot of steaming liquid and cover and simmer for about 30 minutes. The artichokes are done when a knife is inserted into the base and there is no resistance.

Roasted Artichokes

Ingredients

12 baby artichokes

1/4 cup olive oil

1/2 cup dry white wine

2 garlic cloves, peeled & crushed

1 lemon, sliced

bread crumbs

salt and pepper to taste

Rinse the artichokes with cold water and place a bowl of cold water with lemon to the side.

Pull the tough outer leaves off until you get to the pale leaves. As you work with each artichoke, submerge it in the lemon water to keep from turning brown.

Cut off the top of the artichokes and the stems.

Then use a paring knife to cut the green ring above the stem.

Stand the artichoke with stem facing upward and slice in half.

Spoon out the fuzzy choke and discard it.

Toss the baby artichoke halves with the olive oil, garlic, a few lemon slices, salt and pepper in a roasting pan. Add the white wine as you toss.

Cover the pan and let roast for about 20 minutes.

Uncover and stir, letting them continue to roast until brown (10-15 minutes).

Transfer to a serving dish and sprinkle with bread crumbs. Use the rest of the lemon slices to garnish.

French Fries

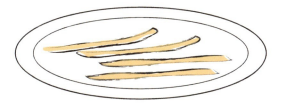

Use your knife and fork in a fine dining situation. In a casual setting you can use your fingers, unless the fries are covered with some sort of sauce. Use your utensils.

Sweet Potato Fries

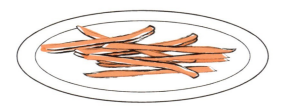

Ingredients

2 lbs sweet potatoes
2 tbsp extra virgin olive oil
1/2 tsp kosher salt
1/2 tsp garlic powder
1/4 tsp paprika

Preheat oven to 450 degrees. Generously coat a cookie sheet with vegetable cooking spray. Wash sweet potatoes and peel. Cut onto 1/2-inch-thick sticks about 4-5 inches long. You can also cut wedges.

Put potatoes, olive oil and seasonings into a large plastic baggie. Toss to coat evenly. Place potatoes in a single layer on cookie sheet. You might need to cook them in two batches. Bake about 15 minutes at 450 degrees. Turn them once and bake another 15 minutes or until done.

Peas

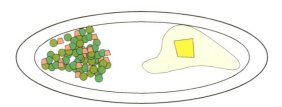

Peas should be slightly crushed with your fork and then eaten with the prongs pointing down. You can actually load something on the fork, such as mashed potatoes, to which the peas will stick.

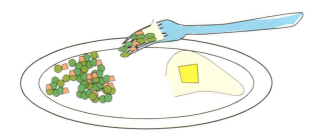

Never scoop your peas like a spoon.

Corn on the Cob

This is a food usually not served in fine dining. But if you happen to be served corn on the cob, pick up the ends with your fingers. Do not use corn holders. That is considered pretentious. Take small bites and do not gnaw into the cob.

Asparagus

Whole spears can be eaten with your hand. To be on the safe side, use your knife and fork to cut them into small pieces. If there is a sauce on the asparagus or if the spears are too long you will embarass yourself by using your fingers.

Roasted Asparagus

Ingredients

1 bunch asparagus
1 tbsp extra virgin olive oil
1/2 tsp garlic powder
salt and pepper to taste
1 tbsp Parmesan cheese
1/2 lemon

Wash asparagus and trim off bottom ends. Preheat oven to 400 degrees. Put olive oil, garlic powder and spears in a plastic baggie. Shake lightly to coat. Arrange on a baking sheet in a single layer and bake until desired doneness, turning once. Transfer to a serving dish and add salt and pepper to taste. Sprinkle with a little lemon juice or zest and Parmesan cheese.

Squash Souffle

adapted from Aunt Fannie's Summer Squash Casserole, Smyrna, Georgia

Ingredients

3 lbs summer squash
1/2 cup onion, chopped
1/2 cup butter, melted
2 eggs, beaten
1 tbsp sugar
1/2 cup bread crumbs
1 tsp salt
1/2 tsp pepper

Wash squash, slice lengthwise and then again in 1/4 inch slices. Put in a pot of water (just covering up to top of squash) with onions. Cook until tender. Drain thoroughly and press out any excess water.

In a mixing bowl, mash the squash and onions together. Add half of your butter, the breadcrumbs, eggs, sugar, salt and pepper. Pour into a casserole or souffle dish and pour the rest of the butter on top. Bake at 375 degrees for 45-60 minutes. The top will turn golden brown.

Green Beans Almondine

Ingredients

1 1/2 lbs fresh green beans
1/4 cup butter
1/2 tsp salt
1/4 tsp savory leaves (cross between thyme and mint)
pinch of oregano
pinch of pepper
sliced almonds

Wash green beans. Break into pieces (optional). Steam until they turn a bright, vivid green. While the beans are steaming, saute sliced almonds with butter, oregano, savory leaves, salt and pepper. Drain and transfer green beans to a dish and pour almondine sauce over them immediately. Toss lightly to coat.

Brussels Sprouts

Ingredients

1 1/2 lbs Brussels sprouts
3 tbsp extra virgin olive oil
1 tsp kosher salt
1/2 tsp pepper

Wash Brussels sprouts thoroughly and put them in a bowl of water. Trim bottom ends and remove yellow leaves. Dry the sprouts and toss them in a plastic baggie with olive oil, salt and pepper. Shake just enough to coat. Pour on a cookie sheet and roast in oven at 375 degrees for 15 minutes. Turn over and roast for about 10 more minutes or until they turn golden brown.

Bon Appétit

Made in the USA
Charleston, SC
30 March 2012